REST
AND
WORK

THEOLOGY OF WORK PROJECT

REST
AND
WORK

THE BIBLE AND YOUR WORK
Study Series

HENDRICKSON
PUBLISHERS

Theology of Work
The Bible and Your Work Study Series: Rest and Work

© 2016 by Hendrickson Publishers Marketing, LLC
P.O. Box 3473
Peabody, Massachusetts 01961-3473
www.hendrickson.com

ISBN 978-1-61970-856-3

William Messenger, Executive Editor, Theology of Work Project
Sean McDonough, Biblical Editor, Theology of Work Project
Patricia Anders, Editorial Director, Hendrickson Publishers

Contributors:

Valerie O'Connell, "Rest and Work" Bible Study
David K. Kim and Leah Archibald, "Rest and Work" in the *Theology of Work Bible Commentary*

The Theology of Work Project is an independent, international organization dedicated to researching, writing, and distributing materials with a biblical perspective on work. The Project's primary mission is to produce resources covering every book of the Bible plus major topics in today's workplaces. Wherever possible, the Project collaborates with other faith-and-work organizations, churches, universities and seminaries to help equip people for meaningful, productive work of every kind.

Printed in the United States of America

First Printing—October 2016

Contents

The Theology of Work

Work is not only a human calling, but also a divine one. "In the beginning God created the heavens and the earth." God worked to create us and created us to work. "The Lord God took the man and put him in the garden of Eden to till it and keep it" (Gen. 2:15). God also created work to be good, even if it's hard to see in a fallen world. To this day, God calls us to work to support ourselves and to serve others (Eph. 4:28).

Work can accomplish many of God's purposes for our lives—the basic necessities of food and shelter, as well as a sense of fulfillment and joy. Our work can create ways to help people thrive; it can discover the depths of God's creation; and it can bring us into wonderful relationships with co-workers and those who benefit from our work (customers, clients, patients, and so forth).

Yet many people face drudgery, boredom, or exploitation at work. We have bad bosses, hostile relationships, and unfriendly work environments. Our work seems useless, unappreciated, faulty, frustrating. We don't get paid enough. We get stuck in dead-end jobs or laid off or fired. We fail. Our skills become obsolete. It's a struggle just to make ends meet. But how can this be if God created work to be good—and what can we do about it? God's answers for these questions must be somewhere in the Bible, but where?

The Theology of Work Project's mission has been to study what the Bible says about work and to develop resources to apply the

Christian faith to our work. It turns out that every book of the Bible gives practical, relevant guidance that can help us do our jobs better, improve our relationships at work, support ourselves, serve others more effectively, and find meaning and value in our work. The Bible shows us how to live all of life—including work—in Christ. Only in Jesus can we and our work be transformed to become the blessing it was always meant to be.

To put it another way, if we are not following Christ during the 100,000 hours of our lives that we spend at work, are we really following Christ? Our lives are more than just one day a week at church. The fact is that God cares about our life *every day of the week*. But how do we become equipped to follow Jesus at work? In the same ways we become equipped for every aspect of life in Christ—listening to sermons, modeling our lives on others' examples, praying for God's guidance, and most of all by studying the Bible and putting it into practice.

This Theology of Work series contains a variety of books to help you apply the Scriptures and Christian faith to your work. This Bible study is one volume in the series The Bible and Your Work. It is intended for those who want to explore what the Bible says about work and how to apply it to their work in positive, practical ways. Although it can be used for individual study, Bible study is especially effective with a group of people committed to practicing what they read in Scripture. In this way, we gain from one another's perspectives and are encouraged to actually *do* what we read in Scripture. Because of the direct focus on work, The Bible and Your Work studies are especially suited for Bible studies *at* work or *with* other people in similar occupations. The following lessons are designed for thirty-minute lunch breaks (or perhaps breakfast before work) during a five-day work week.

Christians today recognize God's calling to us in and through our work—for ourselves and for those whom we serve. May God use this book to help you follow Christ in every sphere of life and work.

Will Messenger, Executive Editor
Theology of Work Project

Introduction

In the first chapters of Genesis, we encounter a God who, despite his infinite power and perfection, takes time to rest. But the Bible begins with work. In an explosion of creation, God creates everything seen and unseen in a magnificent display of work, lovingly and perfectly executed. We watch as God creates people to be similar to him:

> Then God said, "Let us make humankind in our image, according to our likeness; and let them have dominion over the fish of the sea, and over the birds of the air, and over the cattle, and over all the wild animals of the earth." (Gen. 1:26)

Right from the start, God not only works, but he also creates people with a job in mind: responsibility over his creation. The immensity of the task he entrusts to us requires that we be workers. The fact that we are created in God's image indicates that work will not only be a necessity but also a key part of our character.

He also intends his people to be those who rest, after the pattern he models on the seventh day of creation:

> And on the seventh day God finished the work that he had done, and he rested on the seventh day from all the work that he had done. (Gen. 2:2)

As the biblical narrative unfolds, we discover that God's dual invitations to work and to rest serve as a validation of the special bond among God, humanity, and creation.

From the opening pages of the Bible, both work and rest are significant topics—and a rhythm of work and rest continues as an important theme throughout the Bible. In this study, we will trace the theme of rest and work in Scripture as we explore four main topics:

1. Why we need to rest;

2. Why we can't rest;

3. How rest is restored; and

4. How we can rest in faith

May you discover (or rediscover) God's directive not only to work but also to *rest* from your work, finding your physical and spiritual refreshment in him.

Chapter 1

Created for Rest and Work

Lesson #1: Rest Is More than Sleep

> On the seventh day God finished his work that he had done,
> and he rested on the seventh day from all his work that he had
> done. So God blessed the seventh day and made it holy, because
> on it God rested from all his work that he had done in creation.
> (Gen. 2:2–3 ESV)

In these two short verses, the fact that God rested is emphasized
three times. After six days of creation, God looks upon the works
of his hands and pronounces it "very good" (Gen. 1:31). But it is
not until the seventh day that God calls something "holy." When
he does, it is not a person or an object, but a day. It is the day of
rest that he interjects into the time and space of creation. This
day of rest receives the attribution of holiness, which is the very
essence of God's character. The fact that this day of rest is elevated
as holy must be important to our understanding of rest and work,
even though it doesn't always fit our modern values.

Today, many people think of rest as something we have to do so
that we can work. Many of us, if we could, would choose bodies
that would not need to rest. We would use these sleep-immune
bodies to work straight through the week, be more productive, and
make more money. In our society, rest is mostly pragmatic. We
sleep because we must (how many times have you heard some-
one say, or said yourself, "I'll sleep when I'm dead"?). Rest is a
functional necessity, devoid of higher meaning or significance.

We can understand why God works when we look at the magnificence of his creation. But the book of Genesis shows us that God both works and rests. Why does God rest? God, in his omnipotence, clearly does not need to rest for reasons of physical tiredness or exhaustion. He does not sleep (Ps. 121:4), nor does he grow weary (Isa. 40:28). He does not need to rest in order to be more productive. After all, he has already created everything. So clearly there is something more to rest than maintaining energy for the production line.

 Food for Thought

Most of us have no problem seeing work as an admirable undertaking. Who do you most admire in your life? Is it because of what they do or have accomplished? What, if anything, do you know about their *rest* life? Most likely, at times you have been justly proud of your work. But have you ever been proud of your *rest*?

_____

_____

_____

_____

_____

_____

_____

Have you ever before thought about the fact that the first thing in creation that God makes holy is not a person or even an object but a day? Does that realization make you view rest in a new light?

_____

_____

_____

_____

_____

_____

_____

_____

Prayer

Father God,

I come to you with an open heart, ready to learn what you want for me in work and in rest. Please help me to not only learn but also to obey your teachings with a willing spirit.

Amen.

Lesson #2: Rest and Obedience

Genesis 2 doesn't tell us why God makes the seventh day holy, just that he does make it holy. In fact, nowhere in the Bible does God explicitly explain himself on this point. But the concept of the Sabbath, as it is developed throughout the Bible, expands on the subject of rest.

The word *Sabbath* first arises in Exodus 16:23–30. Majestically and miraculously, God's people had escaped Egypt after Moses told them that the Lord had commanded, "Tomorrow is to be a day of sabbath rest, a holy sabbath to the Lord" (NIV). As it was a new concept to these people, not everyone warmed to the idea immediately, and obedience was not unanimous. By Exodus 20, the idea of a Sabbath rest was formalized as it became the Sabbath day, commanded by God in the fourth commandment:

> Remember the sabbath day, and keep it holy. Six days you shall labor and do all your work. But the seventh day is a sabbath to the Lord your God; you shall not do any work—you, your son or your daughter, your male or female slave, your livestock, or the alien resident in your towns. For in six days the Lord made heaven and earth, the sea, and all that is in them, but rested the seventh day; therefore the Lord blessed the sabbath day and consecrated it. (Exod. 20:8–11)

The fourth commandment to remember the Sabbath and keep it holy is grounded upon God's pattern of working six days and resting on the seventh, making an explicit link between creation and Sabbath observance: "For in six days the Lord made heaven and earth, the sea, and all that is in them, but rested the seventh day" (Exod. 20:11). Israel is commanded to rest, because God rests in creation.

The sanctity of rest in no way undervalues the importance or dignity of work. God establishes a pattern of work and rest in which to do one without the other is a deviation from God's created order. The fourth commandment combines a command to work and a command to rest: "Six days you shall labor and do all your work." God affirms both the goodness of work and the sacredness of rest, with the two beautifully woven together.

 *Food for Thought*

God commanded his people to rest as well as work. People naturally work to alleviate hunger, find shelter, and build defenses. But instilling the value of rest beyond the need for sleep required a command. Think for a moment about the ways you naturally treat work and rest. Which comes more naturally to you and why?

_____

_____

_____

_____

_____

_____

What might the God of all creation have done in his time of resting? If you could do absolutely anything, what would give you true rest?

_____

_____

_____

_____

_____

_____

_____

Prayer

Dear God,

I believe you created me to both work and rest. Please lead me to find deeper meaning and refreshment in your rest, as well as purpose and joy in obedience.

Amen.

Lesson #3: Rest and Relationship

The Sabbath is about God's desire to be in intimate relationship with his people:

> "Therefore the Israelites shall keep the sabbath, observing the sabbath throughout their generations, as a perpetual covenant. It is a sign forever between me and the people of Israel that in six days the LORD made heaven and earth, and on the seventh day he rested, and was refreshed." (Exod. 31:16–17)

The Sabbath functions as a sign, pointing to the covenant between God and Israel. This covenant embodies the privileged relationship Israel enjoys with God, a relationship that formally begins with the patriarch Abraham. The Sabbath is also a source of refreshment, a day when God himself is "refreshed," and he wants his people to experience that same refreshment. Keeping the Sabbath is a way of living out the special relationship God's people enjoy with him.

In Ezekiel 20:12, we also see this relational aspect of the Sabbath: "I gave them my sabbaths, as a sign between me and them, so that they might know that I the LORD sanctify them." God gives Israel *his* sabbaths (the refreshment that belongs to him as a relational sign between God and his people), so they might know who he is, as well as the sanctifying effects of relating with him.

The sign is not arbitrary, like a tattoo or a secret gesture. Instead, the sign of the Sabbath is real participation with God in the delight of resting in his own creation. Through this sign, God makes it clear that he chooses not to be distant from his creation—rather that he chooses to intimately commune with his people and with his creation through their participation in his Sabbath rest.

 Food for Thought

It's easy for most of us to think of observing the Sabbath as a commandment, especially if we were regularly dragged to church as less than enthusiastic children. But God says that it is a sign of his perpetual covenant—or perpetual promise and commitment. Think of practices you usually associate with your Sabbath tradition. Are they done under a commandment, or as a response to a promise from God? What differences, if any, do you sense when viewing the same action from these two viewpoints?

_____

_____

_____

_____

_____

_____

_____

_____

When was the last time you felt close to God in your work? When was the last time you felt close to God while resting? Do your current opinions about work and rest, either positive or negative, affect how you relate to God in these areas?

_____

_____

_____

_____

_____

_____

_____

_____

Prayer

    Father,

    Teach me to love your ways and to obey you in all of mine. Help me to understand your rest as a privilege and sign of our relationship. May it deepen and grow to your glory.

                                  Amen.

Chapter 2

When Rest Is Not Restful

Lesson #1: The Fall at Work and Rest

If rest is a source of refreshment and a means to a better relationship with God, as well as with other people, why don't we do it? The answer begins with the fall of humanity:

> To Adam [God] said, "Because you have listened to the voice of your wife and have eaten of the tree of which I commanded you, 'You shall not eat of it,' cursed is the ground because of you; in pain you shall eat of it all the days of your life; thorns and thistles it shall bring forth for you; and you shall eat the plants of the field. By the sweat of your face you shall eat bread, till you return to the ground, for out of it you were taken; for you are dust, and to dust you shall return." (Gen. 3:17–19 ESV)

Adam and Eve's disobedience breaks the intimate fellowship they were intended to have with God, with a result that is devastating to all aspects of creation—including both work and rest. Work, which was originally intended to be an ennobling partnership with God, becomes difficult and painful. Rest, likewise intended to be an ennobling affirmation of humanity's intimate fellowship with God, is deeply distorted. After the Fall, rest becomes a necessary antidote to the harshness of work. But because humanity's perfect relationship with God is broken, rest is elusive.

Work itself is not a curse. Rather, the ground is cursed and that gives rise to pain, frustration, and hardship associated with work. Work itself remains noble and still brings joy, yet because of the

Fall it is now exhausting. In a world that is broken, people rest merely to survive, to refuel for more backbreaking work.

Despite the brokenness that enters the world due to human sin, God's goal is to restore for his people a holy rhythm of work and rest. He does this first by giving the Israelites specific commandments regarding work and rest. Later, God expands the scope and possibility of both rest and work through the life and sacrifice of Jesus.

 Food for Thought

Do you think of your workplace as a place broken by sin? How might it be different if you worked under pre-Fall conditions? Is there any way you can bring rest and refreshment to your workplace or to the people you work with? What might you do to offer rest to others?

_____

_____

_____

_____

_____

_____

_____

_____

On a daily basis, do you experience your work as a curse or as a blessing? In what ways?

_____

_____

_____

_____

_____

_____

_____

_____

Prayer

Jesus,

Please open my eyes to ways I can make my workplace less harsh for others. May you be a source of rest to me and to those around me.

Amen.

Lesson #2: Holidays

Because life outside of Eden is extra hard for humans in their work, God institutes additional cycles of rest into Israel's calendar year. In Leviticus 23, God establishes seasonal festivals and feasts, including the feast of the Passover, a harvest festival, a day for atonement, and a rest day preceding it by a week, as well as the festival of booths.

For each of these festivals, God commands the Israelites to stop their regular work and observe a rest punctuated by specific actions for each festival day. The actions help the people focus on specific aspects of their connection with God. In Leviticus 23:23–25, we see an example of a command to rest and to perform a connecting ritual, in this case on Rosh Hashanah:

> The LORD spoke to Moses, saying: Speak to the people of Israel, saying: In the seventh month, on the first day of the month, you shall observe a day of complete rest, a holy convocation commemorated with trumpet blasts. You shall not work at your occupations; and you shall present the LORD's offering by fire.

For this festival, God commands the people to rest from their normal occupations, and instead to gather together, blow trumpets, and give back some of their earnings to God in the form of a sacrifice. These actions serve to remind them that God is the ultimate provider of both their work and their rest. The fact that God studded the year with commanded rests, sacrifices, rituals, and festivals meant that the Israelites were regularly forced to stop and recognize the passage of time and their reliance on God.

 Food for Thought

For us today, holidays can be more stressful and demanding than even the most hectic day at work. Family obligations, conflicting demands, and over scheduling can take the rest out of our celebrations. What is the difference in your life between holidays and rest? Can you think of ways to make the next holiday more meaningful and refreshing for yourself and for those with whom you share it?

_____

_____

_____

_____

_____

_____

_____

_____

Are there times in the year when you are more likely to slow down and reflect on the important things in your life? Many people dread certain holidays because of loneliness or loss. If you have such a holiday in mind, picture God establishing it as a day that is holy and intended to draw you closer to him. Are there ways you can introduce purpose and meaning into this particular day to turn it into a form of worship?

_____

_____

_____

_____

_____

_____

_____

_____

Prayer

Lord,

I know that every day belongs to you, but I need reminders to bring you into my life. Help me to celebrate the joy of others and to lift the spirits of those who are hurting.

Amen.

Lesson #3: When Rest Doesn't Happen

Ideally, all people would work and rest in comfortable alternation, leaving them physically healthy, mentally stimulated, and spiritually fulfilled. Alas, for many people this happens rarely. Given the busy patterns of their lives, many neglect to rest or do not have the opportunity to rest. With the dizzying advance of technology, people can work anywhere and anytime. This often translates into working everywhere all the time.

Others find their time consumed by the need to earn a paycheck, care for children or aging parents (or both), and fulfill others' needs and expectations. Overworked, they find it increasingly difficult to experience the kind of life-restoring, humanizing rest they need. Conversely, some people are underworked, either for lack of full-time employment or from feeling disengaged from their jobs. Even those who work full time may suffer from a lack of productive engagement, feeling undervalued and unappreciated.

Both conditions—being overworked or underworked—make rest a real challenge. For that reason, people in either of these circumstances may find it difficult to connect with God in the rhythm of work and rest he intended. Unfortunately, there are spiritual implications to a lack of rest.

When people don't rest, they suffer physically, mentally, emotion-
ally, and spiritually. Physical and mental exhaustion can often
lead to emotional volatility, as a poorly rested individual becomes
easily irritated and anxious. This lack of rest can escalate into
larger issues, straining relationships as well as health. Over time,
a person's spiritual life—a connection to God and the deepest
meaning and joy in life—also becomes diminished.

 Food for Thought

Think of two days at work. Day #1: You were flat-out busy from
the instant you walked in the door. Day #2: Nothing good or bad
happened; in fact, the highlight of your day was checking your
watch every ten minutes, convinced either that it was broken or
that time had begun to stand still. Which day is more exhausting
and why? What does being overworked or underworked teach us
about work and rest?

_____

_____

_____

_____

_____

_____

_____

Are you a person who seems incapable of putting down your electronic device? If so, why? Are you afraid that something bad will happen without your attention? Or are you more afraid that life will carry on just fine without you?

_____

_____

_____

_____

_____

_____

Take a moment to examine your relationships with your work, family, and God. Is rest a healthy part of those relationships?

_____

_____

_____

_____

_____

_____

_____

Prayer

Dear God,

Thank you for my work. I see it as a blessing and a provision from your hand to my life. Please help me put this blessing into godly balance with the other blessings before me.

Amen.

Chapter 3

The Many Faces of Rest

Lesson #1: Physical and Spiritual Rest

In addition to the weekly Sabbath rest and observance, God also commands the Israelites to observe patterns of extended rest every seven years (Exod. 23; Lev. 25:1–7) and every forty-nine years (Lev. 25:8–55). These various cycles of rest serve two functions. The first is to give both people and the land physical rest from the hardship and demands of work. The second reason for these rhythmic rests is to invite people to commune with God in worship, satisfying a greater need than just that of their physical bodies.

God's people need physical rest, yes, but they also need a deep spiritual rest—rest from the instability, anxiety, and insecurity created by life in difficult and uncertain circumstances. God institutes these cycles of rest so that his people can set aside time to worship him and rediscover his covenantal love and faithfulness toward them. During these times of worship, Israel is reminded that God himself is their rest: "My presence will go with you, and I will give you rest" (Exod. 33:14).

When Israel turns to God in trust and obedience, this promise of rest is realized through divine protection. Israel is blessed victory over their enemies and possession of the Promised Land:

> And the LORD gave them rest on every side just as he had sworn to their ancestors; not one of all their enemies had withstood them, for the LORD had given all their enemies into their hands. Not one of all the good promises that the LORD had made to the house of Israel had failed; all came to pass. (Josh. 21:44–45)

Likewise, God promises to bless us with rest in his presence.

 Food for Thought

Do you find physical or emotional exertion more draining? Think through a typical week and make a list of the demands on your strengths, resources, and time. Include "hidden" tasks such as paying bills or feeling guilt for not returning phone calls to friends. Are there ways you can lighten your load or turn some obligations into blessings?

_____

_____

_____

_____

_____

_____

_____

How do you find spiritual rest? What gives you respite from anxiety or insecurity?

_____

_____

_____

_____

_____

_____

Prayer

Jesus,

You are God's answer to all of my questions. Quiet my heart to listen to you today.

Amen.

Lesson #2: A Deeper Rest

God gives his people rest from every kind of stress and exertion. Throughout the Bible, there are numerous examples of the rest God gives, including rest from: war (Josh. 11:23; 14:15; 1 Kgs 5:4; 1 Chron. 22:9; Ps. 46:9–10; Prov. 1:33; Isa. 14:3), social strife (Eccles. 10:4; 1 Cor. 1:10; 2 Cor. 13:11; 1 Thess. 4:11; Heb. 12:14; James 3:17–18; 1 Pet. 3:8), fear (Gen. 32:11; Ps. 127:2; Mic. 4:4; Matt. 6:31; 8:24–25; Mark 4:37–38; Luke 8:23–24; 12:29), and anxiety (Matt. 6:25; Phil. 4:6; 1 Pet. 5:7). His presence provides security (Deut. 33:12; Prov. 19:23) and peace even in the midst of death (Deut. 31:16; Job 3:13–17; Rev. 14:13).

God offers a deeper rest that can be described as a spiritual rest—a rest that comes from being in covenantal communion with him. When believers obediently enter this communion, they are invited to enter a deep rest in which there is serenity, peace, and hope. In this state, there is no strife and no fear because this rest is filled with trust in God and reliance on his promises. The reason many people fall short of this rest is because they look to things that are not God to provide rest and security. The result is increased restlessness and a sense that all is not well.

People today are not always aware of the need for both physical *and* spiritual rest. Physical rest without spiritual rest is not satisfying, nor is spiritual rest without physical rest restoring. Keeping the Sabbath holy means recognizing both needs and looking to God to mend both broken bodies and misguided hopes.

 Food for Thought

What kind of rest do you most need today? Is there a type of war in your life? Or is there social strife, fear, or anxiety? What does God promise in regard to this need? Read some of the Scriptures offered above and pray for God to give you rest in this area of your life.

_____

_____

_____

_____

_____

What are the ways you find comfort, solace, or relief from stress? Do your current practices have a positive or negative impact on your peace of mind, body, finances, relationships, or walk with God? Are you pleased with your inventory, or are there ways you could more productively address your need for rest?

_____

_____

_____

_____

_____

_____

Prayer

> *Lord,*
>
> *Meet me today in my anxiety, fear, and strife. You have promised to give me rest. Guide me into your rest today.*
>
> *Amen.*

Lesson #3: A God-given Rest

As we have already seen in Genesis 1:26, God created us to be similar to him:

> Then God said, "Let us make humankind in our image, according to our likeness; and let them have dominion over the fish of the sea, and over the birds of the air, and over the cattle, and over all the wild animals of the earth."

And he created us with a job in mind: responsibility over creation. The immensity of the task he entrusts to us proves that God intends his people to be workers, as he is a worker. In the same way, he intends his people to rest after the pattern he modeled on the seventh day of creation.

The New Testament extends both the directive to enter into God's rest and the possibility of doing so. Hebrews 4:1 encourages Jesus' followers to rest: "Therefore, while the promise of entering his rest is still open, let us take care that none of you should seem to have failed to reach it."

Followers of Jesus receive good news about the rest God promised from the beginning. Because of Christ's sacrifice, believers are able to accept God's offer of rest, regardless of who they are or where they live:

A sabbath rest still remains for the people of God; for those who enter God's rest also cease from their labors as God did from his. Let us therefore make every effort to enter that rest, so that no one may fall through such disobedience as theirs. (Heb. 4:9–11)

These passages convey a deeper significance to rest, communicated by the notion of Sabbath. When rest is "God's rest," it transcends mere recuperation from a hectic, tiring week. In a Christian Sabbath, rest can become the affirmation of a special saving relationship we have with God through Jesus Christ.

 Food for Thought

What kind of rest do you think is meant in Hebrews 4:1? What promises about rest are open because of Jesus?

_____

_____

_____

_____

_____

_____

_____

"A sabbath rest still remains for the people of God; for those who enter God's rest also cease from their labors as God did from his. Let us therefore make every effort to enter that rest, so that no one may fall through such disobedience as theirs" (Heb. 4:9–11). What "effort" to "enter that rest" do you need to make? Why does the writer consider not doing so disobedience?

_____

_____

_____

_____

_____

_____

_____

Prayer

Father God,

Thank you for creating me in your image. I want to rest as you rested. Help me through Jesus Christ, in the power of your Holy Spirit.

Amen.

Chapter 4

Why We Don't Rest

Lesson #1: Distrust Destroys Rest

If we are created to rest and even commanded to do so, why don't we do it? Distrust of God is one of the main reasons we find in the Scriptures. Sadly, distrust among God's people appears early and often in the Bible. An examination of distrust can help us understand why it may be difficult for us to enter into God's rest today.

God demonstrated his faithfulness to the Hebrew people in the wilderness, providing for all their needs as they traveled to the Promised Land. This provision included food in the form of an unknown substance, manna. God specifically instructed the Israelites to collect enough manna for each day, but no more than their need for that day. The exception to this rule was on the sixth day when they were commanded to collect enough for two days, so that they could rest from work on the Sabbath (Exod. 16:4–5).

God's instructions were clear: collect enough food for *each day*— no more, no less—and God would be faithful to provide for them *that day*. After having experienced the miraculous exodus from Egypt, the Israelites had no conceivable reason to believe that God wouldn't provide the food he promised. And yet on the seventh day plenty of people were ready to disobey God, heading out to gather manna that wasn't there.

Did they simply forget it was the Sabbath? No, they failed the test to trust and obey God. Indeed, the threat of testing was explicit in God's instructions:

> Then the Lord said to Moses, "Behold, I am about to rain bread
> from heaven for you, and the people shall go out and gather a
> day's portion every day, that I may test them, whether they will
> walk in my law or not." (Exod. 16:4 ESV)

God recognized the deeper problem within the hearts of his
people—they did not rest on the Sabbath because their hearts
did not trust in God's provision. Neither can we enjoy the rest
God offers unless we trust in the God who offers it.

 Food for Thought

The story of manna is not only a story about bread. It is a tale
of God's faithfulness in the face of humanity's unfaithfulness. It
underscores the relationship between distrust and disobedience.
In what ways do you trust God each day? In what ways are you
less than obedient to his commandments?

_____

_____

_____

_____

_____

Think about the many ways you and those you care about are
provided for, including food, health care, shelter, and education.
Does the degree of provision you experience strengthen your faith
in God? Or do you place more faith in your own efforts?

_____

_____

_____

_____

_____

_____

_____

Prayer

Father,

Give me this day my daily bread. Increase my faith, so that I may come to trust and obey you in all circumstances.

Amen.

Lesson #2: Dissatisfaction Destroys Rest

If distrust is one reason people overwork, then dissatisfaction is another. The author of Ecclesiastes observes that some people work constantly because nothing brings them satisfaction—not their work or the fruits of their labor, not even pleasure:

> I saw vanity under the sun . . . there is no end to all their toil, and their eyes are never satisfied with riches. "For whom am I toiling," they ask, "and depriving myself of pleasure?" This also is vanity and an unhappy business. (Eccles. 4:7–8)

We end up in the "unhappy business" of working to relieve the dissatisfaction in our lives, our loss of relationship with God and others, our fears about not having the things we need, and our inability to find pleasure in anything. Obsessive work makes us only more restless and unhappy. Refusal to rest on the Sabbath stands in the way of God's plan to restore the world from the effects of the Fall. It is a serious offense in the Old Testament, and a problem for us today as well.

God asks, "What is this evil thing that you are doing, profaning the sabbath day? Did not your ancestors act in this way, and did not our God bring all this disaster on us and on this city? Yet you bring more wrath on Israel by profaning the sabbath" (Neh. 13:17–18).

Dissatisfaction and the ceaseless craving for more and better things spell disaster for our health, relationships, and spiritual life. It is true that some people are unable to rest because they are enslaved by external forces, as Israel was when they were in the land of Egypt. But if rest is a possibility for us we should not "profane" God's Sabbath through overwork.

 Food for Thought

Do any of these thoughts sound familiar? "I feel guilty that I'm not working." "I'm afraid other people will get ahead." "I'll lose my job if I don't keep working." "I won't get promoted." "My company will go under if I don't work." "I work because I love what I do." Are there any valid reasons for working without rest?

_____

_____

_____

_____

_____

_____

Work is important to God and to your relationship with him. He wants you to have what you need. How do you draw the line between working to meet your needs and working to satisfy an ever-increasing definition of what "need" means? What part does dissatisfaction play in your work life?

_____

_____

_____

_____

_____

_____

_____

Prayer

Jesus,

When you came into my life, I experienced peace, joy, and gratitude. Please help me to reject dissatisfaction. Your love is enough.

Amen.

Lesson #3: Genuine Need Precludes Rest

Christ makes it spiritually possible for all believers to experience the rest that was previously reserved for Israel. Yet rest is not always fairly distributed in this imperfect world. Many of God's people today lack basic necessities, even the food and water needed to survive. The world is so broken by sin that God's promise of provision is not always fulfilled in this life. It would not be good news to impose an undue burden on people in dire circumstances by commanding them to take a day off from work when such rest is impossible. The Sabbath is intended to be liberation for people, not an added burden.

Jesus performs work to relieve people in need on the Sabbath and teaches that "the sabbath was made for humankind, and not humankind for the sabbath" (Mark 2:27). Christ gives people *freedom* to rest, not an impossible task to fulfill. Jesus shows nothing but compassion for those in distress, healing on the Sabbath and explaining:

> "Suppose one of you has only one sheep and it falls into a pit on the sabbath; will you not lay hold of it and lift it out? How much more valuable is a human being than a sheep! So it is lawful to do good on the sabbath." (Matt. 12:11–12)

For those people currently enslaved either literally or by economic necessity, there is no rule that will allow anyone to judge them for their Sabbath practices. All Christians would do well, rather, to partner with God in his continuing work of liberating the oppressed.

 Food for Thought

What circumstances in your life constrain your ability to rest? Does a commandment to rest feel like a burden or liberation to you?

_____

_____

_____

_____

_____

_____

_____

_____

How do you show compassion for people in distress? Does helping others fall into the category of rest or work for you?

_____

_____

_____

_____

_____

_____

_____

_____

Prayer

Dear God,

Thank you for all you have given me. Please grant me discernment so I can honestly meet my needs and the needs of others.

Amen.

Chapter 5

Free to Rest

Lesson #1: The Lord of the Sabbath and Rest Restored

How can we break out of a destructive, self-centered cycle of working and wanting so that we can experience the rest we need? As much as we might like rest to be a simple matter of strict discipline, it is not. People cannot simply schedule periods of rest into their calendars like a dentist appointment and expect to experience the deep rest of God's Sabbath. Rest is not a matter of scheduling, but a matter of trust in God. It is a matter of the heart. In Matthew 11:28–30, Jesus calls us to rest in him:

> "Come to me, all you that are weary and are carrying heavy burdens, and I will give you rest. Take my yoke upon you, and learn from me; for I am gentle and humble in heart, and you will find rest for your souls. For my yoke is easy, and my burden is light."

This claim infuriated some Israelites because they knew only God could provide that kind of rest, as in Exodus 33:14, "My presence will go with you, and I will give you rest." It was indeed Jesus' intention to identify himself as the one true God who could provide the kind of rest promised to Israel. Jesus made another startling claim when he stated that he is greater than the Sabbath and the temple because he is, in fact, the "lord of the sabbath" (Matt. 12:8).

Jesus provides a greater rest than the law of the Sabbath because, in him, the law is already fulfilled.

> For God has done what the law, weakened by the flesh, could not
> do: by sending his own Son in the likeness of sinful flesh, and
> to deal with sin, he condemned sin in the flesh, so that the just
> requirement of the law might be fulfilled in us, who walk not ac-
> cording to the flesh but according to the Spirit. (Rom. 8:3–4)

On its own, the Sabbath law has no ability to give rest. It teaches
that people ought to rest, but it cannot enable them to do so. In
Jesus, we are freed from sin and empowered by the Spirit to experience deep spiritual rest.

 Food for Thought

Jesus' image of carrying heavy burdens is at first a physical one,
reinforced by the notion of a yoke used for farm animals. But
he also promises rest for the soul. If you have burdens, are they
physical or spiritual?

_____

_____

_____

_____

_____

_____

_____

In what way is the rest that Jesus provides superior to the weekly rest commanded in the Old Testament?

_____

_____

_____

_____

_____

_____

Prayer

Jesus,

I give you my heavy burdens. May I work in partnership with you and find rest for my soul.

Amen.

Lesson #2: Freed to Rest

Often we desire to be self-sufficient without God. We think that freedom from accountability will make our lives more enjoyable. Yet the effort that it takes to live this way leaves us exhausted and empty. God wants to commune with his people through his rest, but we can't commune with a God we fear.

Jesus frees us from condemnation by forgiving all sin through his sacrifice on the cross. In doing so Jesus grants Christians renewed access to God that individuals could never earn or accomplish on their own. No longer estranged from God due to sin, we can now enter into real, restful communion with God.

The Christian faith, as laid out in the letters to the early church, clearly states that Christ fulfilled the law and gained freedom for his people. In Christ, we are saved from the condemnation we deserve under the commandments and requirements of the law:

> There is therefore now no condemnation for those who are in Christ Jesus. For the law of the Spirit of life in Christ Jesus has set you free from the law of sin and of death. For God has done what the law, weakened by the flesh, could not do: by sending his own Son in the likeness of sinful flesh, and to deal with sin, he condemned sin in the flesh, so that the just requirement of the law might be fulfilled in us, who walk not according to the flesh but according to the Spirit. (Rom. 8:1–4)

Because we no longer need to be afraid of God, we are also freed from the need to work incessantly in a futile attempt to please God. In this way Jesus' sacrifice makes true rest possible.

 Food for Thought

By establishing forgiveness, Jesus reconciles each person's relationship with God. In what ways does forgiveness shape your daily experience of life, work, and rest?

_____

_____

_____

_____

_____

_____

Paul assures us, saying, "For I am convinced that neither death, nor life, nor angels, nor rulers, nor things present, nor things to come, nor powers, nor height, nor depth, nor anything else in all creation, will be able to separate us from the love of God in Christ Jesus our Lord" (Rom. 8:38–39). According to this passage, we should be able to experience a restful relationship with God, despite real-world obstacles. What circumstances in your life make rest difficult or work unpleasant? Do they impact your experience of God?

_____

_____

_____

_____

_____

_____

_____

_____

Prayer

Jesus,

Thank you for freeing me from sin and condemnation. Help me to experience the joy of my salvation in both my work and my rest.

Amen.

Lesson #3: Adopted to Rest

Through Christ's sacrifice, the parent-child relationship between God and his people is restored:

> For you did not receive a spirit of slavery to fall back into fear, but you have received a spirit of adoption. When we cry, "Abba! Father!" it is that very Spirit bearing witness with our spirit that we are children of God, and if children, then heirs, heirs of God and joint heirs with Christ—if, in fact, we suffer with him so that we may also be glorified with him. (Rom. 8:15–17)

Jesus reinstates all the privileges and benefits of being a child of God—privileges that God gave to Adam and Eve in the Garden of Eden. Adopted as God's children, we have every right to ask him for what we need, knowing he will not withhold any good thing from us (Rom. 8:32; 2 Cor. 9:8).

Having God as our Father does not negate the possibility of suffering in the life of a Christian. The world is still fallen, and God has the eternal view in mind. In some ways, suffering can be seen as taking part in the family business. We sometimes have the opportunity to suffer with God in the same way that Jesus comes alongside all people who are suffering. Whether believers feel extremely provided for or extremely in need, Jesus' sacrifice means they no longer have to turn to their own work as the ultimate source of security and identity. They are loved, and they are not alone.

When we partner with God in his work of restoration and reconciliation, the Holy Spirit helps us deepen our relationships with God and with others. The gift of the Holy Spirit (John 16:7) makes it possible for followers to give their time and property sacrificially to others (Acts 4:34). God's very Spirit empowers us to live by faith, to work by faith, and finally to rest in faith.

 *Food for Thought*

In Matthew 7:10, Jesus asks a crowd if any one of them would give his hungry child a snake when he asked for a fish. Without waiting for the obvious answer, in verse 11 he concludes, "If you then, who are evil, know how to give good gifts to your children, how much more will your Father in heaven give good things to those who ask him!" Describe below the best parent-child relationship you know. Does God parent you in the same way? If so, how?

_____

_____

_____

_____

_____

_____

God not only created you, but he also chose to adopt you through Jesus Christ. On the basis of God's word, you are twice chosen and loved. What sort of rest do you imagine God wants for his children?

_____

_____

_____

_____

_____

_____

Prayer

Dear God,

How often I call you "Father" without thinking of what that means. I ask that your Holy Spirit enliven the spirit of adoption in me through Jesus Christ.

Amen.

Chapter 6

The Sabbath Today

Lesson #1: Are Christians Required to Observe a Sabbath Day?

Jesus' sacrifice gives Christians the freedom to enter into God's rest on a perpetual basis. So the natural question is whether a practice of keeping a weekly day of rest, referred to in the Old Testament as the Sabbath, is necessary for Christian believers. The Apostle Paul clearly seems to give each Christian the freedom to choose the answer to this question:

> Some judge one day to be better than another, while others judge all days to be alike. Let all be fully convinced in their own minds. Those who observe the day, observe it in honor of the Lord. Also those who eat, eat in honor of the Lord, since they give thanks to God; while those who abstain, abstain in honor of the Lord and give thanks to God. (Rom. 14:5–6)

Some Christians interpret this passage as a reason for doing away with a formal Sabbath day altogether, but Romans also clearly states that those who choose to keep a Sabbath should not be judged for it. Whether a believer sets aside a specific day for Sabbath, or rests only as the spirit leads, this passage from Romans indicates that both practices should include thanking God.

Although people are free to choose when and how to rest, there are compelling arguments both for observing a weekly Sabbath rest and for worshiping collectively with other Christians on a customary day of the week. Throughout the history of the church, Christians have widely observed some sort of weekly meeting involving worship. Jesus' own disciples certainly went to the temple on the Jewish Sabbath, if for no other reason than to convince others that Jesus is the Messiah (Acts 17:1–4).

In his own life, Jesus demonstrated two distinct practices of Sabbath, engaging in personal spiritual rest as well as communal worship experiences. Jesus took moments alone to rest in God's presence (Matt. 14:13), often returning to use the Jewish Sabbath worship for reaching out to others with his message of salvation (Luke 4:16–21). Since both resting personally and worshiping communally were important in the life of Jesus, modern Christians might do well to make similar choices with their God-given freedom.

 Food for Thought

Do you regularly observe a day to abstain from work and to worship God? Why or why not?

_____

_____

_____

_____

_____

_____

_____

When you think of the weekly worship services available to you, do you consider them an obligation or an opportunity?

_____

_____

_____

_____

_____

_____

_____

_____

Prayer

> *Lord,*
>
> *You give all good things to me, including the freedom to worship you. Help me to do so with great joy.*
>
> *Amen.*

Lesson #2: The Rest of Others

Christians, freed from the law, have no legal requirement to celebrate the Sabbath on a particular day, but a general call to worship and serve God. With today's technology, we can study the Bible at home, listen to wonderful sermons on demand, and pray at will. Yet we still cannot do communal worship on our own.

Whether or not people choose to rest in a particular weekly pattern, those who manage other people have a responsibility to ensure that workers reporting to them have proper access to rest. God's commandment to the Israelites reveals his deep concern for the rest of all people:

> But the seventh day is a sabbath to the LORD your God; you shall not do any work—you, or your son or your daughter, or your male or female slave, or your ox or your donkey, or any of your livestock, or the resident alien in your towns, so that your male and female slave may rest as well as you. Remember that you were a slave in the land of Egypt, and the LORD your God brought you out from there with a mighty hand and an outstretched arm; therefore the LORD your God commanded you to keep the sabbath day. (Deut. 5:14–15)

In this passage, the end of slavery brings freedom to rest—that is, a break from unceasing work. Our freedom to observe the Sabbath in a manner of our choosing must always be seen in this light. Because God delivered the Israelites from slavery in Egypt, he expects his followers to deal fairly with others. Furthermore, Jesus' sacrifice of his own life is not limited to one religious group but "for many" (Matt. 26:28). When managers protect rest time for employees, they can view this management practice as partnering with God in his continual work of deliverance.

 Food for Thought

Providing for the rest of workers may take different forms. A telecommunications company based in North Carolina has a policy that everyone should leave work by 6:00 p.m. in order to spend dinnertime with the people they love. If necessary, people may work from home after 8:00 p.m. or so, but workers are expected not to work or communicate with one another at least between

6:00 and 8:00. What are some positive outcomes this policy might have on the business, employees, and their families? Can you think of any negatives?

_____

_____

_____

_____

_____

_____

_____

Think of your own workplace. How do you use your position to provide rest for those with whom you work? Is there anything you can do to actively promote the restful well-being of your customers and colleagues?

_____

_____

_____

_____

_____

_____

_____

Prayer

Lord,

Let me never forget that I too was once a slave in the land of Egypt. May I extend your rest and blessing to all I meet.

Amen.

Lesson #3: The Future of Rest

We know that Christ will come again one day to fully restore God's original intention for his creation—and that includes both work and rest. In today's fallen world, we will always be subject to a pattern of frustration and exhaustion. But when Christ comes again to make the world the way God has always intended it to be, he will reestablish an integrated pattern of purposeful work in partnership with God and rest in perfect communion with him. The following passage from Revelation features themes of both work and rest:

> The angel said to me, "Write this: Blessed are those who are invited to the marriage supper of the Lamb." And he said to me, "These are true words of God." Then I fell down at his feet to worship him, but he said to me, "You must not do that! I am a fellow servant with you and your comrades who hold the testimony of Jesus. Worship God!" (Rev. 19:9–10)

Life in the new creation will involve work (in fellow service with the angels) and rest (enjoying the marriage supper of the Lamb). Human work and rest in the age to come will both occur in perfect partnership with God. Believers who eagerly await this time can experience closeness with God today in their work and rest (Heb. 4:1).

Until Jesus returns, it is important for us to examine whether our current rhythms of work and rest bring us closer to peaceful communion with God or further away from it. In the Old Testament, God instituted various patterns or cycles of rest, creating regular rhythms for the Israelites. Though Jesus' sacrifice frees Christians from the need to follow the Mosaic Law in all its details, the weekly, monthly, seasonal, annual, and sabbatical rhythms of rest can provide useful guidelines for those who want to enter into the freeing rest that Christ's finished work makes possible.

 Food for Thought

Rest communicates the character of a holy God who relishes the act of creation (Prov. 8:30–31) and who wants to commune with it. Rest is the gracious outworking of God's desire to be in intimate, joyful relationship with humanity and creation. Therefore, it is not surprising that both work and rest will be part of the new world. Looking forward to that time, in what ways do you think work and rest will be different from today?

_____

_____

_____

_____

_____

_____

_____

Take an inventory of the various ways you worship God. Do you observe regular times of worship daily, weekly, or yearly? Which increases your enjoyment of worship: regularity or spontaneity?

_____

_____

_____

_____

_____

_____

_____

_____

Prayer

Lord Jesus,

Come into my world today. Teach me to serve and worship you in the strength and refreshment of your Holy Spirit. Let my work honor you and my rest please you.

Amen.

Chapter 7

The Christian at Rest

Lesson #1: The Mind at Rest

Many barriers to rest start in the mind. It is particularly difficult to rest when life circumstances create resentments against others, fear of the many things that can go wrong, or anxiety about others' expectations. Thoughts that are angry, resentful, or anxious prevent rest. The writer of Hebrews reminds us to let go of distractions, looking instead to Jesus, with trust in him for the future. Our example is Christ himself, who faced the cross with a focus on the joy to come.

> Let us also lay aside every weight and the sin that clings so closely, and let us run with perseverance the race that is set before us, looking to Jesus the pioneer and perfecter of our faith, who for the sake of the joy that was set before him endured the cross, disregarding its shame, and has taken his seat at the right hand of the throne of God. (Heb. 12:1–2)

This freedom to fix active thoughts on Christ, and in particular a future hope of glory, can be found throughout the letters of the New Testament.

> Finally, beloved, whatever is true, whatever is honorable, whatever is just, whatever is pure, whatever is pleasing, whatever is commendable, if there is any excellence and if there is anything worthy of praise, think about these things. (Phil. 4:8)

Philippians exhorts us to think about whatever is good and true and beautiful. Colossians 3:1–4 encourages us to imagine the glorious future that awaits all those who look to Christ.

Second Corinthians 4:17–18 invites us to accept current problems and difficulties as momentary afflictions compared to the eternal rest that awaits us. Christians who choose to follow this advice can enter into God's rest and the peace that passes all understanding. To rest fully is to anchor the mind upon Jesus and the perfect future that awaits all who follow him.

 Food for Thought

A critical part of experiencing deep rest is being proactive about what thoughts fill the mind. When you are bombarded constantly by images of lust, fear, hatred, and insecurity, how does this affect your thinking and your ability to rest?

_____

_____

_____

_____

_____

_____

_____

Prepare yourself now to take command of your mind. Think about things you find pure, pleasing, commendable, excellent, and worthy of praise. Write down as many as you can.

_____

_____

_____

_____

_____

_____

_____

Prayer

> *Holy God,*
>
> *I want to see Jesus in the world around me. Help me to focus on things that are true, just, and pure in my work today.*
>
> *Amen.*

Lesson #2: Rest in Repentance

Entering into a faithful rest involves examining existing desires. Jesus invites "all who are weary" to come to him for rest (Matt. 11:28). But coming to Christ is not a casual or passive decision.

Jesus makes clear that being his disciple is a life-consuming reality that requires self-denial, which doesn't come naturally to us:

> Then Jesus told his disciples, "If any want to become my followers, let them deny themselves and take up their cross and follow me. For those who want to save their life will lose it, and those who lose their life for my sake will find it. For what will it profit them if they gain the whole world but forfeit their life? Or what will they give in return for their life?" (Matt. 16:24–26)

Many people don't experience true rest because they pursue something that promises rest but can't ever deliver it. We may feel superior to those who worship idols because we don't bow down to golden images. But the Bible views anything that we pursue above or in place of God as an idol. We pile up entertainment and achievements, hoping to climb high enough to numb the fear of failure or lack of purpose. Even good things can become idols when they take the place of Christ.

We instinctively look to these things to provide a sense of deep rest, but idols all fail at some point. Idols keep us from trusting God and cause us to forfeit the grace that brings true rest. God invites his followers to rest amid work, but idols require ever-increasing frenzy with ever-decreasing satisfaction and reward.

Breaking this vicious cycle to overthrow idols and return Christ to the center of our lives requires repentance. In repentance, each individual surrenders the illusion of control, dying to a false sense of self-sufficiency.

You are invited to trust that God can and will graciously provide for all the "desires of your heart" (Ps. 37:4). In repentance you find you can trust God to give you rest.

 *Food for Thought*

God wants you to rest and to be free of anxiety. When the stresses of your week catch up with you, what do you do to unwind? Looking at each approach you use, thoughtfully consider if it is healthy, harmful, or neutral in your life.

_____

_____

_____

_____

_____

_____

_____

Repentance means turning toward God if you have taken a wrong turn in the past. Are there any areas in your work that warrant repentance?

_____

_____

_____

_____

_____

_____

Prayer

Father,

I come to you in the name of Jesus to ask that your Holy Spirit bring to my mind any idols, activities, habits, or desires that stand between us. I ask for your good gift of deep repentance and joy.

Amen.

Lesson #3: The Christian Sabbath

Personal rest practices vary greatly, as do people themselves. One person's idea of a restful afternoon might easily be another's equivalent of a forced march in the desert. God delights in diversity. Whatever rest practices we choose should serve to pull us as individuals into a deeper experience of God's faithfulness.

God gave the weekly Sabbath to the Israelites to provide them with rest and to remind them of his never-ending, faithful provision. Jesus healed on the Sabbath to demonstrate his dominion over all problems and his ascendency over all religious structures, commands, and traditions. Therefore, any particular approach we take to observing a Sabbath rest—whether attending a church service, reading a devotional, or sharing a meal with family or friends—should be undertaken with God's intended purposes in mind.

As Christians who are not bound by intricate Sabbath requirements, we need to take care that our own Sabbath practices remain filled with worship and gratitude. Just as rest is more than sleep, so the Sabbath observance is more than an absence of labor.

Here are some practical suggestions for those of you looking to release your burdens to Jesus and enter into God's rest. The list is simple and basic, intended to prompt your thinking rather than to compel your action:

1. Reflect on things that are just, pure, and excellent (Phil. 4:8). Train your mind to turn from fearful thoughts to whatever brings you hope and joy. Some find it helpful to keep a gratitude journal.

2. Imagine a future that transcends the current problems of this world (Col. 3:1–4). If the new world of Revelation were to begin tomorrow, what would be different? How might you be different? How can you start today?

3. Reframe your current troubles as small within an eternal timescale (2 Cor. 4:17–18). Imagine looking at a current situation from a distant future time point (also known as a "fast-forward" model of decision making). If this task seems too difficult, remember a time in your life when a problem seemed insurmountable or a broken heart unrecoverable. How does it look to you now?

4. If you're relying on a solution that promises to fix all life's problems, and it's not Jesus, repent of it and move on.

5. Reflect on whether adding daily rest practices might be helpful to you, or if they would become just another stressful demand. Examples include reading a daily devotional book or following a Bible reading plan, praying worshipfully at the beginning and end of every day, or praying together with family members at an evening meal. Whatever you do, do it with a grateful and hopeful heart, not as a dry exercise in going through motions of holiness.

6. Reflect on weekly rest practices that feel refreshing. Some people commit to one full day of rest a week, or to a weekly meeting of a small group of Christians. Many people find a weekly church service refreshing and a source of connection in an increasingly isolated society. And if you go to a weekly service, don't go only to receive something for yourself; look for ways you can contribute as well. You may find giving your time and talents to be a surprising source of renewal and refreshment. Although weekly worship services are a hallmark of Christian life, it isn't the high-water mark of Sabbath rest. The condition of the heart and relationship with God is the spirit of that rest.

7. Many weekly rest ideas are considered to be rest because they are fun, including enjoying a meal with friends and neighbors, playing or listening to music, engaging in a recreational activity, intentionally and joyfully spending time with your family, or serving others in need.

8. Discover rest practices that help you focus on special aspects of God, either seasonally or annually. Spend extended times in prayer or reading Scripture. Go on a retreat. Celebrate holidays or seasons of more intensive spiritual devotion, such as Advent and Lent.

9. Place a high value on rest—yours and that of others. Find ways to prayerfully rest in small ways as well as big. Lunch breaks and commuting time can bring rest, as well as annual vacations and weekly Sabbath celebrations.

10. Place a high value on all of your time—work and rest—considering them as gifts from a loving God: "So teach us to count our days that we may gain a wise heart" (Ps. 90:12).

 *Food for Thought*

Prayerfully review the list of rest practices above. Which suggestions attract you and why?

_____

_____

_____

_____

_____

_____

_____

No Christian needs to feel condemned for forgoing a weekly Sabbath observation. However, there are many benefits to keeping this practice. What are your thoughts now regarding the question of Christians and Sabbath?

_____

_____

_____

_____

_____

_____

_____

Prayer

Heavenly Father,

Thank you for your rest and for the love that offers it to me. Teach me to find you in both work and rest.

Amen.

Conclusion

The biblical narrative of work and rest is a rich and complex story. From the very beginning, work is "good" and rest is declared "holy" when God sanctifies the seventh day, setting it apart from the others. God creates because it is his nature, he rests because he delights in it, and he shares both with the people he created.

In its original design, work was intended to be an ennobling partnership between God and his people, with rest serving as an invitation to fellowship. God's dual invitations to work and to rest reflect the special bond between God, humanity, and creation.

The repercussions of the Fall make work difficult and create a desperate need for both physical and spiritual rest. Today many find rest especially challenging in a world of always-on communication demands.

Although the challenge to rest is modern, its origins are ancient. Meeting with Moses atop Mount Sinai, God instituted a mandatory day of rest for his people through the Sabbath observance in the fourth commandment:

> "Therefore the Israelites shall keep the sabbath, observing the sabbath throughout their generations, as a perpetual covenant. It is a sign forever between me and the people of Israel that in six days the LORD made heaven and earth, and on the seventh day he rested, and was refreshed." (Exod. 31:16–17)

The Sabbath rest was foundational to the development of Israel as a covenantal people. Violation of that command constituted separation from God and from Israel, with death a realistic outcome.

The fourth commandment, as recalled in Deuteronomy, supported the rhythm of work and rest with an additional argument based on God's deliverance of his people out of Egypt:

> "Remember that you were a slave in the land of Egypt, and the Lord your God brought you out from there with a mighty hand and an outstretched arm; therefore the Lord your God commanded you to keep the sabbath day." (Deut. 5:15)

God's ordered rhythm of work and rest mirrors his model in creation and in redemption.

But, as soon became apparent, the law is powerless to offer rest, let alone change hearts. Calling himself "Lord of the sabbath," Jesus underscored the notion that the Sabbath was created for humanity and not the other way around. As Christians who are freed from the law through the all-sufficient sacrifice of Jesus, we are also freed from the requirement of observing a strict weekly Sabbath rest. Christians are free to rest or work, in any combination, on any given day.

But our freedom does not negate the rhythms of creation or the purposes of God in all we do. People still need rest—both spiritual and physical—a rest that goes far deeper than mere sleep. We are also called to worship in private and in community with other believers. The fact that so many Christians have chosen to continue in the tradition of weekly Sabbath observance is instructive. It is an encouragement for each one of us to join in the many opportunities to give, as well as to receive, in this rich celebration of God and his creation.

We've spent most of our time considering how we as individuals and as followers of Jesus Christ can best understand and act on

God's loving command to observe a rhythm of work and rest. We are called to do this because we are built to need it, invited to share fellowship in it, and reminded of God's deliverance as we do so. But the Bible also asks us to look out for others who need rest. Consider how you might do this in your sphere of influence. Maybe there is an overworked single mother in your neighborhood who could use a couple of hours of time to herself—time that you could give her by watching her children.

Perhaps you know an elderly person who is wearied by the unbroken stretch of loneliness—loneliness you could lighten with a refreshing visit. A hardworking father injured at work may have to go weeks without a paycheck before disability insurance kicks in—a modest check or a bag of groceries would lift the weight of hopelessness.

There are so many needs, great and small, all around us. Each offers us the opportunity to come alongside our Father to bring rest to a broken world in the spirit of the Lord of the Sabbath.

 Food for Thought

As we conclude our study of rest and work, take a moment to consider whatever God has brought to your attention during this time. What have you learned—about God or about yourself? Has your view on your own rhythm of rest and work changed?

_____

_____

_____

_____

_____

_____

_____

_____

Will you be doing anything different from now on? What new rest practices will you take on or leave off? Take a moment to prayerfully consider what God wants you to take away from this time you have invested in learning about him.

_____

_____

_____

_____

_____

_____

_____

_____

Prayer

Lord,

Thank you for giving me a heart to learn more about you. I ask that in my work and in my rest, I will honor you, doing both as daily forms of worship in gratitude for your love.

Amen.

Wisdom for Using This Study in the Workplace

Community within the workplace is a good thing and a Christian community within the workplace is even better. Sensitivity is needed, however, when we get together in the workplace (even a Christian workplace) to enjoy fellowship time together, learn what the Bible has to say about our work, and encourage one another in Jesus' name. When you meet at your place of employment, here are some guidelines to keep in mind:

- *Be sensitive to your surroundings.* Know your company policy about having such a group on company property. Make sure not to give the impression that this is a secret or exclusive group.

- *Be sensitive to time constraints.* Don't go over your allotted time. Don't be late to work! Make sure you are a good witness to the others (especially non-Christians) in your workplace by being fully committed to your work during working hours and doing all your work with excellence.

- *Be sensitive to the shy or silent members of your group.* Encourage everyone in the group and give them a chance to talk.

- *Be sensitive to the others by being prepared.* Read the Bible study material and Scripture passages and think about your answers to the questions ahead of time.

These Bible studies are based on the Theology of Work biblical commentary. Besides reading the commentary, please visit the Theology of Work website (www.theologyofwork.org) for videos, interviews, and other material on the Bible and your work.

Leader's Guide

Living Word. It is always exciting to start a new group and study. The possibilities of growth and relationship are limitless when we engage with one another and with God's word. Always remember that God's word is "alive and active, sharper than any double-edged sword" (Heb. 4:12) and when you study his word, it should change you.

A Way Has Been Made. Please know you and each person joining your study have been prayed for by people you will probably never meet who share your faith. And remember that "the LORD himself goes before you and will be with you; he will never leave you nor forsake you. Do not be afraid; do not be discouraged" (Deut. 31:8). As a leader, you need to know that truth. Remind yourself of it throughout this study.

Pray. It is always a good idea to pray for your study and those involved weeks before you even begin. It is recommended to pray for yourself as leader, your group members, and the time you are about to spend together. It's no small thing you are about to start and the more you prepare in the Spirit, the better. Apart from Jesus, we can do nothing (John 14:5). Remain in him and "you will bear much fruit" (John 15:5). It's also a good idea to have trusted friends pray and intercede for you and your group as you work through the study.

Spiritual Battle. Like it or not, the Bible teaches that we are in the middle of a spiritual battle. The enemy would like nothing more than for this study to be ineffective. It would be part of his scheme to have group members not show up or engage in any discussion. His victory would be that your group just passes time together going through the motions of a yet another Bible study. You, as a leader, are a threat to the enemy, as it is your desire to lead people down the path of righteousness (as taught in Proverbs). Read Ephesians 6:10–20 and put your armor on.

Scripture. Prepare before your study by reading the selected Scripture verses ahead of time.

Chapters. Each chapter contains approximately three lessons. As you work through the lessons, keep in mind the particular chapter theme in connection with the lessons. These lessons are designed so that you can go through them in thirty minutes each.

Lessons. Each lesson has teaching points with their own discussion questions. This format should keep the participants engaged with the text and one another.

Food for Thought. The questions at the end of the teaching points are there to create discussion and deepen the connection between each person and the content being addressed. You know the people in your group and should feel free to come up with your own questions or adapt the ones provided to best meet the needs of your group. Again, this would require some preparation beforehand.

Opening and Closing Prayers. Sometimes prayer prompts are given before and usually after each lesson. These are just suggestions. You know your group and the needs present, so please feel free to pray accordingly.

Bible Commentary. The Theology of Work series contains a variety of books to help you apply the Scriptures and Christian faith to your work. This Bible study is based on the *Theology of Work Bible Commentary*, examining what the Bible say about work. This commentary is intended to assist those with theological training or interest to conduct in-depth research into passages or books of Scripture.

Video Clips. The Theology of Work website (www.theologyofwork .org) provides good video footage of people from the marketplace highlighting the teaching from all the books of the Bible. It would be great to incorporate some of these videos into your teaching time.

Enjoy your study! Remember that God's word does not return void—ever. It produces fruit and succeeds in whatever way God has intended it to succeed.

> "So shall my word be that goes out from my mouth;
>   it shall not return to me empty,
>   but it shall accomplish that which I purpose,
>   and succeed in the thing for which I sent it." (Isa. 55:11)

"This commentary was written exactly for those of us who aim to integrate our faith and work on a daily basis and is an excellent reminder that God hasn't called the world to go to the church, but has called the Church to go to the world."

BONNIE WURZBACHER

FORMER SENIOR VICE PRESIDENT, THE COCA-COLA COMPANY